Too Perfect for This Life

A mother's story of faith, hope and healing through grieving the loss of her son

Becky Beck

What Matters with Becky Beck

Praise for Too Perfect for This Life

What a beautiful, heartbreaking, faith promoting story about a mother and family that goes through such a difficult trial, but never give up, and never forget what keeps them standing. Thank you for sharing your story and your faith! What a sweet reunion you will have with your baby Kevin.
—Cookee6

Heart filled love faith and hope. Anyone needing to know or feel the love of their Savior, Jesus Christ, through life's trials, this is the perfect read to boost you up, knowing we all have a loving Savior to carry us through. —J. Jeppson

Beautifully written. Both a heartbreaking and an uplifting story of hope, loss, courage, faith and family. —Amazon Review

Must read for parents who have lost a child due to birth complications. —Amazon Review

Inspirational memoir of a dedicated mother. —Dee

I was really touched by this sweet book. Kevin Jr. couldn't have been born to a better family than the Beck family, your Christlike example has made me want be a better person. I could not put this book down, the Spirit was so strong, and my tears just flowed as I felt your deep sadness as well as the Savior's love. Becky, thank you for sharing this tender experience. I highly recommend this sweet and gospel oriented book. —Marsha

I believe that Becky's story would be helpful for anyone struggling to make sense of a similar diagnosis and the grief that comes along with it. She is honest and real in describing her feelings. Although Becky is a person of faith I think it would also be a meaningful read for those who don't share her beliefs or who might make a different decision than she did. It's thoughtful, reflective, and heartbreaking, but it's also full of love, peace and hope. —Cynthia

Dedicated to all my favorites

Kevin, Jackson, Emmy, Dakota, Kloe, Gracie, Janie,
Lilly, Kevin Jr and Jesus

Contents

Prologue

The Phone Call

I t was Monday January 2nd, 2012. I can still picture myself sitting on the floor of our bedroom. We'd just gotten home from a week long visit with my brother Rob's family in Arizona. My husband, Kevin, was with me and we were both completely exhausted from driving straight through the night. I was trying to muster up the energy to unpack, when my cell phone rang. I didn't recognize the number, but assumed it was Fetal Fotos calling to remind me of my appointment for the next day. It was a follow up from our initial ultrasound we'd had on December 24th at 18 weeks pregnant. The technician wasn't able to completely confirm the baby's gender, so she wanted us to return a week or two later.

BECKY BECK

When I answered the phone, a girl from Fetal Fotos was on the other end of the line, however, she wasn't calling to confirm the second appointment. "Our doctor reviewed your ultrasound, and he found a problem with the baby's head. He recommends you contact your doctor for an ultrasound."

"Oh, well several of my babies have had big heads, they run in the family," I responded.

"No...," she hesitated, "It's not actually the head, but the face. It's the width of the face that isn't right." I thanked her for the information and hung up the phone. I repeated the conversation to Kevin; we were both confused, but quickly convinced ourselves it was just a precaution. We agreed to wait for the ultrasound with my midwife later that week before jumping to any conclusions.

1

Another Girl

I met Kevin at the beginning of our ninth grade year at Valley Junior High School. We had our first class of the day together and quickly became great friends. At the beginning of our Sophomore year Kevin took me on our first date to Taylorsville High School's Homecoming Dance and we've been together ever since. We had a long distance relationship for two years while I went away to Rick's College in Idaho and he served a full time mission in Oklahoma for The Church of Jesus Christ of Latter Day Saints. We wrote each other faithfully and were married six months after he returned home.

I remember asking Kevin when he wanted to start a family. I'll admit his response, "As soon as possible," surprised me a bit. I was alright with that, but for me, *as soon as possible* was after I graduated from Utah State University, which wouldn't be for another year. We thought we'd have around four children and I wanted to be done having babies by the time I was 30. We became pregnant with our first child in June of 1993. The baby was due the day after I was to graduate with my bachelor's degree in Elementary Education.

My water broke on President's Day February 21st, 1993 around 3:00 a.m. About six hours later we had a baby boy. He surprised all of us, arriving three weeks early and weighing six pounds twelve ounces. He was born with quite the cone head, which my mom assured me was only temporary. We named him Jackson Thomas, after my dad, Thomas Dee Sollis. It was just me and Kevin in the delivery room and he was the perfect coach. I'd been anxious and scared of childbirth throughout my pregnancy, so I was pleasantly surprised by how much I loved giving birth, and experiencing all of it with Kevin at my side. I also loved that epidural. It seemed so easy, and I remember thinking, *I could totally do this again.*

It took me awhile to get the hang of the mom thing. I had to go back to school and finish my last two weeks of student teaching when Jackson was a week old. I hated leaving him. Our mom's were great to help, each taking a week to come up to Logan from Salt Lake to watch Jackson while Kevin worked and I taught my class of sixth graders. It was a long, stressful two weeks. I was still recovering from childbirth, my hormones were all over the place, trying to figure out how to nurse was hard, and I got a bad case of mastitis. But I powered through and was able to graduate with a Bachelor of Science in Education.

Adjusting from full time student to full-time mommy was hard. It took me a while to really bond with Jackson. It didn't come as easy as I thought it would, but in time I found my stride and I fell head over heels in love with my sweet baby boy. Jackson and Kevin became my whole world and I loved taking care of them. When Jackson was about two and a half years old we welcomed our second child. My sister Natalie joined us for this birth and filmed the entire delivery. We didn't know the sex of our first three babies because Kevin thought not knowing would be a fun surprise, and he was right. I had always wanted a girl, so when Dr. Macy held up our baby, I was beyond excited to see we had a daughter! We named her Emmy Diana after two of my grandmothers. Emmy after my dad's mother, Emma (all the grandkids called her Grandma Emmy), and Diana after my Grandma Emmy's sister, Diana, whom I called Grandma Dee Dee because she'd always been like a grandmother to me.

My mom joined us for the birth of our third child, Dakota Reed. Kevin knew a cute little boy on his mission named Dakota, and Reed was the name of his grandfather, Reed Atwood Beck. I delivered him natural and it was rough. I was not prepared for that kind of pain, and my mom and Kevin weren't prepared to watch me experience that kind of pain. Mom told me afterwards, "I don't think I'll be coming to any more of your births."

"If you ever have another natural childbirth I won't be coming either," Kevin agreed.

Following Dakota's birth, I experienced some issues with my heart and terrible daily headaches. For a while I thought maybe our family was complete. Around the time Dakota turned two I kept having this nagging feeling that we had another baby waiting, so I finally talked to Kevin about it. Busy and overwhelmed with starting a new business, his initial response was, "This is the worst possible time."

He was right, the timing wasn't great, and although my heart was better, my headaches continued to be really bad. Still though, I couldn't deny what I'd been feeling, so I prayed that God would soften Kevin's heart towards the idea. About a week later he came to me and said I was right; he agreed it was time to have another baby and assured me all the other things would work themselves out.

Our fourth child, Kloe May, was born two months before Dakota's third birthday and three months before I turned 30. It was a smooth and easy birth. We arrived at the hospital at 1:00 p.m., I received an epidural around 2:00 p.m., and Kloe May, named after Kevin's father's mother, Billie May Beck, was born about an hour later. She was the perfect baby: a great sleeper, great eater (which was obvious as she was such a chubby little thing), and always so happy and content. I felt like I was getting pretty good at mothering, it was no longer as overwhelming as it had been with the first three. The older children were great helpers and my headaches improved some, so I was open to the idea of having one or two more. I became pregnant with our fifth child when I was 32.

Gracie Anne was born three weeks early, just like most of our babies. We gave her my middle name. She gave us a scare when she couldn't breathe and had to be life-flighted by ambulance to Primary Children's Hospital the day after she was born. She was diagnosed with pneumonia and spent ten days in the NICU. Just a few days after we brought her home, I had an overwhelming feeling that there was a baby boy waiting to come to our family. It was so strong that I felt as if his spirit was in the same room with me. I welcomed the idea of another son and assumed he would be our sixth child and we would be done.

I have always been blessed when it comes to getting pregnant. We've been able to plan each of our babies, and the plan was to have our sixth child around the time I turned 34. Knowing the additional risk of complications once I turned 35, I didn't want to wait. A year passed, then another. After about two years of trying, I finally got pregnant. We were all so excited and ready for another little one.

There would be four years between Gracie and this baby. With my other pregnancies I was never completely out of the baby phase, so this time it felt as if I was starting over. We began thinking about boy names. Kevin and I have an agreement: he chooses the boy names and I choose the girls, except we both have to agree on whatever name is chosen. I gave him all kinds of suggestions: Logan, Lincoln, Solomon (we'd call him Sollie for short after Grandpa Sollie, my dad's father). Kevin didn't seem to like any of them, and he wouldn't give me any suggestions.

At my 20 week ultrasound the entire family came, every one of us expecting to find out it was a boy. The radiologist had no trouble seeing the sex of the baby. "It looks like you are definitely having a girl!" she told us. I knew she had to be mistaken. She printed us some pictures and sure enough, it was obvious our son was, in fact, a daughter. I left the ultrasound completely confused and a little embarrassed. I had told everyone about "our boy," and now I had to tell them I was wrong...but I couldn't shake the feeling that I wasn't.

BECKY BECK

I believe God has a plan for our family and what
it should look like and I didn't want to leave anyone
out. If I was right, that would mean I needed to have
another baby, but that felt impossible. I was 36 and,
in my mind, too old to be having babies. My body
was feeling like it would barely make it through this
pregnancy, let alone another one. I finally decided
to pray about it. I asked God if the feelings I'd had
about another boy were right, or had I misinterpreted
them? I told God I was willing to have another baby.
I just needed him to tell me what he wanted me to
do. Several weeks later, I was sitting in church when
my answer came. We had another girl and a boy who
needed to join our family. The answer was clear, and I
was grateful to know. I also knew God would help me
do it. I shared my answer and my feelings with Kevin
later that night. At first, he was frustrated at the idea
of another baby. I knew he was already overwhelmed
with the responsibility of providing for all of us. As we
talked, his heart softened and although he didn't fully
understand, he trusted what I knew, and we settled
into the idea of having one more. From that day on,

my pregnancy got easier and I could feel the Lord giving me the strength I needed to get through it.

BECKY BECK

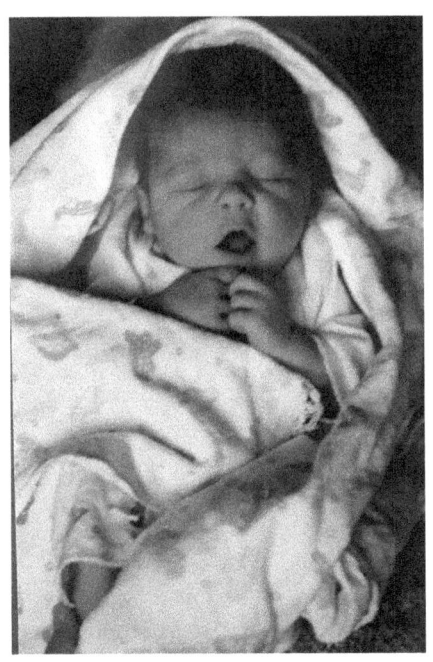

BECKY BECK

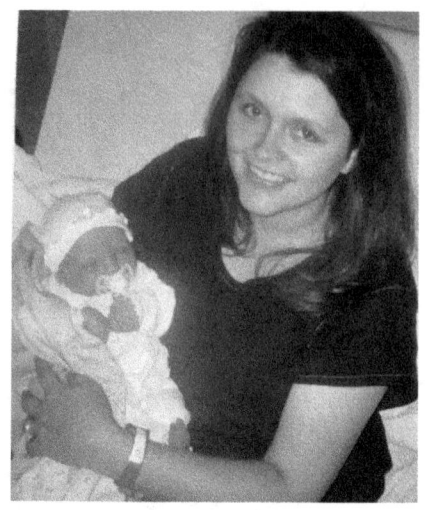

2

Janie Rose

Our Janie Rose was born September 18th of 2008, sandwiched nicely between her sisters Gracie and Kloe, whose birthdays are September 16th and 20th. Their Dad's birthday is is September 24th, so needless to say, September is the party month for our family! When I was pregnant with Janie, there was a time when Kevin and I were doing sealings in the Jordan River Temple. In our church we build temples to make promises and receive blessings from God and also to seal families for eternity. We receive these blessings and make these promises for ourselves and for those who have passed away before receiving their temple blessings—if they choose to accept them. One of the daughters we sealed to her family that day was named Janie Rose. As soon as we heard the name, we both knew that was the name we'd give our daughter.

There has never been, in the history of the world, a baby more spoiled and loved than Janie Rose. She had three extra little mothers, two adoring brothers, and a dad who she had wrapped around her finger from the moment he saw her. Dad and Janie spent a lot of time together since Kevin was working from home. He was such a big help with Janie and all the kids. Having six children seemed easier than back in the days when we had only two or three, so shortly after Janie's first birthday we started trying for "our boy." About eight months later we got pregnant.

3

A Beautiful, Perfect Baby

We were paying cash for our seventh baby, so I shopped around for the best priced hospital and doctor. I remember going in for my first appointment with Dr. Barney. The nurse asked me about all my previous pregnancies. She wanted to know how many live births I'd had, how many miscarriages, how many pregnancies with complications, and the names and birth dates of all my children. As I listed the details for each child and then watched her tally the results; it totalled six live births, zero miscarriages and zero complications. The nurse was impressed, and I was grateful. I knew I'd been blessed when it came to carrying babies. I often tell people that having babies is my thing. Some women run marathons, others paint, some like to cook. I have babies. It's what I do.

The day before our 20 week ultrasound I told Kevin, "Just so you know, I'm sure this is the boy we've been waiting for, but in case I'm wrong, I'm willing to try one more time."

Kevin came unglued, "It is ridiculous to keep having babies until we get a boy, we can't be having babies into our 50's." He was clearly frustrated, so I changed the subject.

This baby was due in March of 2011 and our 20 week ultrasound was scheduled the morning of October 22nd, 2010. It was just Kevin and Gracie attending this time. We sat in the waiting room for what seemed like forever. We were surrounded by pregnant women, most looked to be younger than myself. I was so nervous. I always have a little worry in the back of my head that they might see a problem with the baby, but this time I was mostly nervous about what we'd see between the two tiny legs.

My name was finally called, and we headed back to one of the little ultrasound rooms. Our radiologist welcomed us, and I immediately liked her. I guessed her to be around my mom's age and she seemed as excited for our ultrasound as we were. She asked the usual questions, how many children we had, boy to girl ratio, and their ages. With four girls and two boys she had no trouble guessing what we were hoping for. This baby was not shy and gave us a clear shot of "the parts" right away. "I'm sorry but this is clearly a baby girl, I have no doubt", the radiologist told us. I felt terrible that she used the words, *I'm sorry*. Boy or girl, it shouldn't matter. And it didn't matter, I was grateful for another daughter. But still very, very confused and a little worried about Kevin's reaction. Kevin absolutely adores his girls, but all their drama and emotion wear him out. On the day of Janie's ultrasound, he came home and went right to bed—it was the middle of the afternoon.

The radiologist went on to examine our daughter. She just kept saying over and over, "This is a beautiful, perfect baby." She did a careful scan of her brain and heart, took measurements of her head, her belly and her limbs. She was a beautiful, perfect baby. But even with this great news, I left the hospital confused and upset. I was meeting a friend for lunch and cried throughout the entire 30 minute drive. They weren't tears of sadness, but rather tears of frustration. I questioned my ability to interpret answers to prayer. I was frustrated with myself for being upset we weren't having a boy, because I knew another healthy baby girl was wonderful. As I drove and cried, I prayed for clarity and understanding and then worked to pull myself together in time for lunch with my friend Shelley.

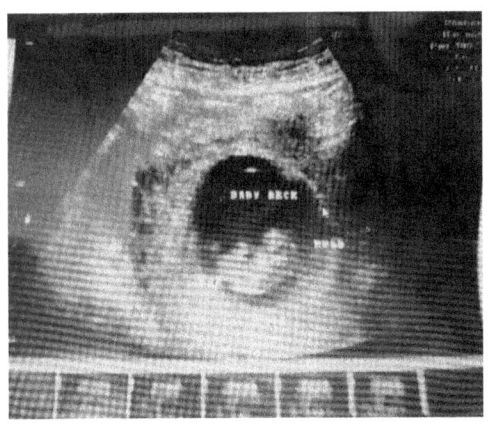

4

Lilly Rebecca

Later that night I pulled a pan of brownies out of the oven with the word "GIRL" written on top in pink sprinkles. A few of the kids seemed a little disappointed it didn't say "BOY," but they quickly got used to the idea and were excited to have another sister. I was still confused with my feelings about having a boy. I continued to pray for understanding and to know God's will. As I thought back on the answers I'd been given, I realized I'd misinterpreted the answer I'd received in church while I was pregnant with Janie. I was told I had another girl and a boy. I assumed "another girl" meant Janie, when it actually meant another girl—in addition to Janie. That realization brought me peace.

Throughout the rest of the pregnancy I didn't talk to Kevin any more about having a boy. We both looked forward to meeting our baby girl. In the meantime, I prayed God would soften Kevin's heart and help him to know as I did, that we still had another son. We began talking about girl names, I liked Amelia and we'd call her Mia or Millie. Jackson didn't like Millie, he said it was short for Mildred and Mildred sounded like an old lady. Sophie, Sadie, and Annie were also on the list, but in the end, the only name everyone liked and agreed upon was Lilly. On February 26th, 2011 at 10:47a.m. Miss Lilly joined our family.

Since Dakota, it had only been me and Kevin at our births. We invited my sister Megan, who's a photographer, to join us for Lilly's birth. I had seen some great examples of birth photography done by my cousin's wife and I loved that so many aspects of the baby's birth could be documented. It was Megan's first birth and she did a wonderful job capturing all the special moments. One of my favorite pictures from that day is of Kevin talking to Lilly. Right after our babies are born Kevin puts his face close to theirs and talks softly to them. They settle right down as their Daddy whispers how much he loves them and how happy he is to meet them. I'd never had a picture of this moment, until Lilly.

We had a hard time settling upon a middle name for Lilly. We like to name our children after a family member, but all our options didn't seem to fit. While we were still in the hospital, Kevin announced to me, "I know what Lilly's middle name should be." He told me he'd been thinking earlier that day about all the great women we've named our girls after and then got a little emotional as he told me, "It only seems fitting that we should name one after you." I had never considered giving one of our girls my name as a first or middle name because of our last name. But Lilly Rebecca Beck will probably lose the "Beck" when she marries some day and it meant a lot to me that he wanted one of our daughters to have my name.

During our second night in the hospital we had a quiet moment. As we were enjoying our Lilly and her sweet little spirit, it felt right to bring up the subject of another baby. I asked Kevin how he felt and told him I was willing to be done if that was what he wanted. I was so grateful for his response, "I trust your feelings and I am willing to try again, especially if it's what God wants us to do." He went on to say, "The timing doesn't matter, so what if Jax is 18 and away at college or on his mission when we have this baby. So what if we're in our 40's."

I felt a sense of relief wash over me. I was so grateful for his support. I have learned time and time again that this life is about sacrifice and obedience to our Heavenly Father and trusting His will. As we are faithful and patient, God opens the windows of heaven.

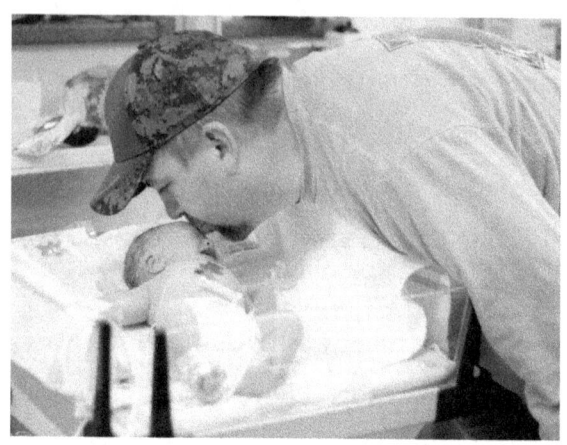

5

Babies in My 30's

I often think how grateful I am that I didn't stop having babies at 30, like I'd planned. I've always loved being a mother, but getting a little time and experience behind me made having babies in my 30's a wonderful thing. I better understood that sleepless nights are temporary, babies eventually grow out of the fussy stage (although it takes some longer than others), and before you know it, they are too big to be rocked and held.

While pregnant with Lilly, I was hoping she would have Kloe's temperament. I thought I was due for another "easy" baby. But our Lilly was just the opposite, she was my hardest. She was fussy and uncomfortable more than she wasn't, and she didn't like anyone to hold her except me and her sister Emmy. I would rock her most of the day, and then when Emmy got home from school, she'd take over so I could get some things done. During this time, I got a glimpse of what a great mommy Emmy will be. She loved her baby sister and was so patient with her. She looked forward to her "Lilly" time every day after school.

We eventually found out Lilly had "silent reflux". I felt so bad for the poor baby. I know how painful reflux is for an adult, so I could only imagine how miserable Lilly was. A baby like Lilly would have put me right over the edge had she been one of my first few children, but thankfully I had acquired a lot of patience and I knew she'd grow out of it.

Lilly's first summer was rough. I had a fussy baby to take care of and a house full of kids who needed me. On top of that, I was battling repeated breast infections. I tried to quit nursing a few times, but my body has no idea how to regulate its milk supply. I produce too much milk and haven't been able to stop nursing until my babies are at least six months old.

As the summer progressed, I began thinking about when to get pregnant again. I didn't want to wait too long. My 40th birthday was fast approaching and with my biological clock ticking, I felt a push to do it sooner than later. But with Lilly still so needy, I wasn't ready to start trying.

6

Perfect Timing

It was September 20th, 2011, Kloe's 10th birthday. I was a week late and decided to take a pregnancy test. I assumed it would be negative since Lilly was only seven months old and still nursing. I picked up the stick and just stared at the faint blue line in the "pregnant" window, wondering to myself, how did this happen? The timing didn't make any sense. I am like a clock; I know when I can get pregnant and when I can't. I counted the months to when this baby would be due. Fifteen months between Lilly and this baby. Fifteen months! My closest babies were two and a half years apart and I prefer at least three years between babies. As I sat alone in the bathroom thinking things through, I realized Jackson would have a few more months with us after the baby was born before going away to college. Our entire family would be together under one roof, not for long, but I'd take it. The overwhelming feelings creeping in on me were quickly replaced with gratitude and excitement. Our baby boy was on his way, I just knew it, and I was far more equipped to handle two babies than I'd ever been before.

I am a planner. I plan my day, my week and my month. I love to plan vacations, projects around the house and I've planned for a lot of babies! Within minutes of finding out I was pregnant I made plans to keep the baby a secret until my birthday when we would be far enough along to find out if it were a boy or a girl. I debated whether or not to tell Kevin, but the odds of keeping it a secret from him were virtually impossible. Besides, I needed someone to talk to about the baby, and Kevin has always been great to sympathize with me through the first few months of being exhausted and nauseated.

I found out we were expecting on a Tuesday, and on Friday of that same week, our date night, Kev and I headed to Bountiful to watch Jackson play football.

For several miles I kept going over in my head what I would say to break the news. I finally just blurted out, "I'm pregnant." I could see by the look on his face he was blindsided.

"No...no...no," he responded.

I assured him repeatedly that it was true. I then proceeded to explain how perfect the timing was, and that his fear of having kids when his kids were having kids could be put to rest.

"Boy or girl, this has to be it," he stated firmly. I agreed.

Often times, the things we don't plan and the challenges and changes God places in our path can become our greatest blessings. I knew within weeks of that day in September when I found out about the baby that God was aware of me and blessing me to be able to handle the toll it was taking on my body and my ability to care for the rest of the family. By October, Lilly had become a new baby. She was much happier, started to really take to her dad and the rest of her siblings, and became the best sleeper! She slept 10-12 hours at night and took two long naps during the day. It allowed me to get plenty of rest and do what I needed to around the house and for the family.

Keeping the baby a secret for over four months was one of my greatest accomplishments. I have my inner circle of a few people besides Kevin that I share special things with. I avoided talking to all of them. It was fall and then winter, so hiding my belly didn't prove to be too difficult. Those were happy, peaceful months and I enjoyed every minute of being pregnant. I didn't even mind the nausea that began around 10 in the morning, continued throughout the day, and was the worst at night. I enjoyed taking care of my husband and my big and little babies, including the one growing inside me. I loved that our entire family was together.

I was still nursing in October. I'd never been pregnant and nursing at the same time and began to wonder if continuing to nurse Lilly would take away from what the baby needed. I did some research and found that the only one that might suffer a little was me, if I didn't eat right. I thought I might try to keep nursing, but then another breast infection hit, and I was done. I began thinking about switching to formula with this baby because with so many infections, nursing Lilly had been frustrating.

7

I Hope it's a Boy

I t was my 40th birthday, December 24th, 2011. All nine of us gathered for breakfast around a large table in the dining room at Little America when we announced to the children that we were expecting another baby. They all stopped eating and just sat there for several seconds. I could see each one of them trying to process this new information. Their questioning looks soon turned to smiles and Kloe said right out loud, "I hope it's a boy!"

Later that afternoon my oldest daughters, Emmy and Kloe, came with us to Fetal Photos to find out the sex of the baby. We were all so excited and a little anxious. It was no secret we were all hoping for a boy. I'd been given an ultrasound at 10 weeks and everything looked great. At 18 weeks I was finally over the nausea and the pregnancy was feeling just like all my others. The ultrasound tech covered my belly with gel and went to work. Right away we saw a busy little baby doing somersaults and throwing kicks and punches. She seemed to have trouble at first getting a clear shot between its legs. Kevin and I had seen our fair share of girl parts so when she finally got a look, we were certain this baby was not a girl. The girl doing the ultrasound wasn't as confident and ended up telling us there was an 80% chance it was a boy. She went on to take several pictures. One of his face, a leg, a foot, and one of his little hand. She scheduled a follow up appointment for January 3rd, hoping to confirm the baby was for sure a boy.

As I went through the pictures on the drive home, I noticed it looked as if the baby had six tiny fingers. I showed Kevin and Emmy and they agreed. It looked like there were six, but surely the girl doing the ultrasound would have said something if that were really the case.

We'd kept the pregnancy a secret from everyone, so I sent out a text message to our family and friends,

"Thanks for all the birthday wishes...for my 40th birthday I got an ultrasound and it looks like there's an 80% chance a BOY will be joining our family in May!" Pretty much everyone I sent the message to was surprised, especially since Lilly was only 10 months old. They replied with well wishes and excitement that we were finally getting our boy!

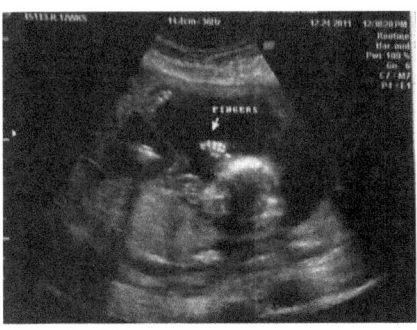

8

Three Areas of Concern

T he call from Fetal Fotos telling us there was
something wrong with our baby's face came on
a Monday. My appointment for the ultrasound with
my midwife was on Thursday, just three days later. I
kept telling myself the doctor at Fetal Fotos was being
overly cautious and whatever he saw on our little guy's
face wasn't anything to worry about.

Kevin and I went into my 20 week ultrasound
with the midwife feeling anxious. I mentioned to
Stephanie, the girl doing the ultrasound, what Fetal
Fotos had told us. Her response was basically that we
can't trust much of what they said since they aren't
technically a medical practice. Stephanie was pretty
quiet throughout the ultrasound. She commented

about how good his spine looked and carefully examined his brain and heart. She said his heart sounded good and then confirmed that we were having a boy. She mentioned his cute little feet and hands—one of them he kept in front of his face. I had begun to wonder over the past couple of days if he had a cleft lip and maybe that was the reason for Fetal Fotos' concern. Stephanie made repeated passes over his face. I kept hoping and waiting for her to say he had no cleft lip and that everything looked normal, but his little hand was always in front of it, sometimes he was even sucking his thumb. She finished and sent us to the waiting room until Tina, my midwife, called us back for the exam. While we waited I sent out text messages letting everyone know that the 80% probability we were having a boy was now 100% and that everything looked good. I assumed everything looked good because we hadn't been told otherwise.

Fifteen minutes passed, then thirty, before my name was finally called. "There are a couple of things we are concerned about with your ultrasound." Tina said as soon as we were all seated. A feeling of panic began rising in my stomach. She continued, "There are three areas of concern. We see bilateral calcification in the ventricles of his heart. I've seen babies with calcification in one ventricle but not both." Just as I was beginning to breathe she added, "Also, one side of his brain has a large dark space which could be excess fluid, but I don't know. I'm not sure what this means for your baby and I would like you to see a specialist." She continued speaking slowly and I could hear the concern in her voice. "And then there is still the question with his face, which we couldn't get a good look at." She left the room to get me a referral form for the specialist. Kevin and I just looked at each other, and I tried not to cry. We went into the appointment worried about his face and now we hear there are problems with his heart and brain as well. I felt blindsided and a little betrayed by Stephanie for not telling me what she was seeing during the ultrasound.

I was sent home with a paper with the words written across the top, *MATERNAL FETAL MEDICINE REFERRAL FORM*. It included a section labeled *REASONS FOR REFERRAL* with the box *Abnormal Ultrasound Findings* checked. She had also written "abnormal cerebral findings, bilateral calcification on ventricles and R/O cleft" (which meant "rule out" cleft). At the bottom of the page it had my appointment time for the following Monday, January 9th, at 11:00 a.m. The entire drive home I just kept telling myself everything would be okay. Whatever his problems were, they could be fixed. I reluctantly sent out another text message to family and close friends about the ultrasound findings. Everyone was concerned, many prayers were offered, and a family fast was organized for that coming Sunday. In our faith we fast for two meals, usually breakfast and lunch, on the first Sunday of every month, and occasionally on other days when we need extra help from heaven. We fast for our family's needs, for friends who are struggling, and often in gratitude for our many blessings. We donate the money we would have used to buy food and other necessities, to help those in our neighborhood who are struggling. I had seen so many blessings come from obeying the law of the fast and I knew it was a resource that could help.

Throughout the weekend I kept thinking about the confirmations I'd received over the years that this baby boy needed to come to our family. Those thoughts brought me a lot of comfort, and I knew I had to put my trust in God and His plan for our son. Initially, I resisted the urge to google the words *abnormal cerebral findings, bilateral calcification on ventricles, and cleft lip.* I had googled various health symptoms before, and more often than not came away with more information than I needed or wanted to know. However, by Saturday night my curiosity got the best of me. I went to the office in our basement where I could be alone. I opened Kevin's laptop and began searching the internet for possible answers. I hoped so much that I could find information that pointed toward a positive outcome. I wanted to find something that would give me hope.

The main word that came from my search was Trisomy. Specifically, Trisomy 13, Trisomy 18 and Trisomy 21. There were images of babies and a few children who had been born with these conditions. Trisomy 21 is also known as Down Syndrome. I knew the increased risks of having a Down Syndrome child at my age and I was alright with that possibility. I would have even welcomed it, so the images of the Trisomy 21 children were not upsetting to me at all. I wasn't, however, prepared for the images of the Trisomy 18 and especially the Trisomy 13 babies. Trisomy 13 babies often have deformities in their faces, and I knew there was no way my baby could have such a severe chromosomal defect. I shut the computer and left the office in complete denial. I spent the rest of the weekend telling myself things weren't as bad as they seemed.

Sunday morning I was up early to put a roast in the crockpot and go over my Sunday School lesson. I'd had a restless night with concerned thoughts and feelings about the extent of what the problems were with the baby. We began our family fast the night before. I wasn't sure what specifically to fast for. I wanted to ask God to bless us with a healthy baby boy, but at the same time, if God's will was different, I trusted Him and wanted whatever He wanted for our baby.

It's incredible to me how much love I could feel for someone I'd never met. I loved my little guy so much and wanted to be able to love him, raise him, and see the effect he would have on the rest of our family. I've loved watching each of our babies join us and be welcomed and spoiled by their siblings, extended family, and friends. Within days of their birth, it's hard to imagine what life was like without them. As I went over the notes for my lesson, my mind kept wandering. I was considering asking Kevin for a priesthood blessing. About five and a half years prior, during a time when I was really struggling, my dad gave me a father's blessing. My sister Megan was there and took notes for me. His blessing was a great comfort to me back then and has continued to provide additional direction and comfort over the years. I opened to the back of my journal, unfolded the sheet of paper and reviewed the words of my dad's blessing. Among them were, *I bless you with peace of mind, the Savior's ultimate peace and I admonish you to put your mind at ease and live one day at a time.* As I read the words, once again I was comforted and knew I was going to be okay. I no longer felt like I needed a blessing, but I did have the strong feeling that our baby did. I decided I'd ask Kevin and my dad to give me a blessing later that day for the baby.

When I arrived at church, many of my friends were anxious to congratulate me. This was the first time we'd been to church since announcing we were expecting again. It was awkward to say, "Thank you," and then follow with, "It looks like there are problems with the baby's heart and brain." The look on their faces quickly changed from excitement to concern and then they'd assure me that everything would be okay.

My lesson that day was entitled, All Things According to His Will. One of the themes of the lesson was finding gratitude even in our struggles. That hit home to me and I was determined to be grateful and not feel sorry for myself, no matter what challenge lay ahead. Later that night, my dad and Kevin placed their hands on my head to give me and the baby a priesthood blessing. Both my father and Kevin are Melchizedek priesthood holders in our church which gives them authority from God to give blessings for healing, comfort, and encouragement. Dad gave the blessing and it was beautiful. He reminded me of our eternal family unit and blessed the baby that he would be strong and healthy through Christ. He blessed me with wisdom to understand, patience, to trust in the Lord, and that through Christ all things are possible. The blessing left me with the impression that our baby boy would have the health and strength to fulfill his mission on earth. How long or short that would be, I didn't know.

MATERNAL FETAL MEDICINE REFERRAL FORM   OBSTETRIX MEDICAL GROUP

PLEASE COMPLETE THE FOLLOWING INFORMATION, CHECK THE APPROPRIATE BOXES,
SIGN THE FORM AND FAX ALONG WITH THE REQUESTED MEDICAL RECORDS TO 801.743.4705.

Requesting Provider: Tina Fought, CNM
Requesting Provider Phone: 801-964-3865   Fax: 801-964-3894
Patient Name: Rebecca Beck   Phone: 801-918-5632
Patient DOB: 12/24/71   Patient EDC:
Referring Physician Signature: T. Fought CNM WHNP   Date: 1/5/12

SERVICES REQUESTED: (Please check all that apply)

- Consultation   ☐ First Trimester NT Screening   ☐ Endovaginal Ultrasound for Cervical Length
- Standard Screening Obstetrical Ultrasound
- "Targeted" Obstetrical Ultrasound for Detailed Fetal Anatomy   Abnormal Cerebral findings
- Non-Stress Test with AFI/ Frequency: bilateral calcifications on ventricles
- Biophysical Profile (BPP)/ Frequency: R/o clep
- Umbilical Artery Doppler Ultrasound/Frequency:
- Middle Cerebral Artery Doppler Ultrasound/Frequency:
- ☐ Amniocentesis   ☐ Chorionic Villous Sampling   ☐ Fetal Blood

9

The Diagnosis

O n the morning of January 9th, I went about my usual routine starting with our family scripture study and prayer at 6:30 a.m. Kevin offered the prayer, asking God to be with us throughout the day and to please bless our baby. I went to work making six sack lunches, and then got myself and the little girls ready. I sent everyone off to school and then spent a few minutes on my knees asking for God to bless me and our baby with the strength to handle whatever was coming. I expected to feel anxious but was grateful for the peace and calm I felt.

At 10:30 a.m. I dropped Janie and Lilly off to my mom and picked up Kevin from school. He'd gone back to college a year earlier to get his associate degree.

He didn't care much for college the first time around, back when we were newly married. I was happy to see that he was enjoying school, for the most part. As we drove together to see the specialist, I tried to remain hopeful and optimistic, pushing all fears to the back of my mind. Kevin and I talked the entire way. I think he was doing his best to distract me. I don't remember what we talked about, but I felt better knowing he would be there with me.

We arrived at St Mark's hospital and held hands as we entered the radiology waiting room in the adjoining office tower. We saw two different radiologists who both performed extensive ultrasounds on the baby. The first radiologist didn't say much as she looked at our baby's heart, brain, face, and other organs. Then the specialist came in to take a look. The discussion that followed was a realization of my worst fears. We had one sick baby boy. Our son had a bilateral cleft palate, severe brain abnormalities and heart problems. I'm sure she gave more specific terms, but I couldn't think, I was suddenly numb and I had such a hard time processing what she was saying. She told us those three markers all pointed towards Trisomy 13 or Trisomy 18, which were both very serious chromosomal defects. I was familiar with the term Trisomy 18. My best friend Marci had a baby girl with Trisomy 18 who died in utero at around 16 weeks. Most Trisomy 18 and 13 babies don't make it to term and those who do, only live a few hours. She went on to explain that if by some chance there wasn't a chromosomal defect, he would be severely mentally disabled. I had so hoped to come away with better news. I was devastated.

The specialist left for a few minutes, and my sweet husband knew just what to say. He looked me in the eyes and said, "It will be okay, you did your part in being faithful and obedient to the promptings to have this little boy. Giving him a body is all that is required of you." His words brought me comfort. I knew he was right, but inside my heart was breaking. As soon as I could, I escaped to the bathroom and completely lost it.

Later that night I couldn't sleep, and I couldn't stop crying. It felt so strange that my baby had so many problems, yet my pregnancy felt so normal. Because he was so active, it was hard to imagine him being so sick. I wrote in my journal that night at 3:00 a.m.

I trust my Heavenly Father completely. I trust in His plan for me and my family and I trust I'll be able to raise this baby in the next life, but the human part of me is having a really hard time...I'm sad for not being able to raise another little son in this life. I've pictured him with our family for so long. On the other hand, my heart is full of gratitude to my Father in Heaven for the opportunity to be the mother of one of these special spirits, and I'm all the more grateful for these seven beautiful healthy he's blessed me with.

10

Choosing a Name

O ver the next few days, the outpouring of love and concern from our family and friends was amazing. Despite the devastation we felt, we also felt a peace in our home. I felt a love from my Heavenly Father and Savior that I'd never experienced before. I'd never felt them so near. I always knew they loved me, but during that time they carried me. They helped me have the strength to get out of bed each morning so I could continue taking care of my family. I still had a husband and seven children that needed me, and the last thing I wanted to do was check out.

We decided that our boy needed a name as soon as possible. We usually don't name our babies until the day they are born, but this baby was different. Every day we had with him was a gift and we wanted the kids to get to know their brother and build a relationship with him while he was still with us. We had talked about some names, but Kevin would never commit to any. My first choice was that he be named after Kevin, Kevin David Jr. I liked that name for Lilly, when we thought Lilly was a boy, but Kevin didn't. So, I was really happy when Kevin came to me and said he'd like to name our baby after him. The kids liked it too, but were concerned about the confusion of their dad and brother having the same name, so we decided we'd call him Baby Kevin.

The specialist told us it was very likely our baby would pass away at any moment. For a short time I constantly wondered, *Would this be the day?* I felt like a ticking time bomb, and I hated the ongoing feeling of being anxious. My concerns soon faded however, as in a quiet moment God blessed me with the assurance that I would carry Baby Kevin full term and the pregnancy would go smoothly, much like my others.

I did a pretty good job of continuing with my day to day responsibilities. When I felt like crying, I cried.

But I mostly cried when I was alone, so as not to upset our kids. I knew they were hurting too. I remember taking Kloe downtown for an errand and the entire drive she asked me questions about the baby. "Where will he go when he dies? Will I be able to hold him when he's born? What is the Plan of Salvation?" It was a sweet experience to be able to explain to her that we all lived as spirit children with our Heavenly Father before this life. We talked about how the purpose of this life is to get a body, to learn and grow, and to have experiences that will help us become more like our brother Jesus Christ. We discussed how when we die, our spirits go back to live with our Father in Heaven. She knew the basics, but now that she was faced with the very real probability that her baby brother would die, it made that plan very real to her and she wanted to better understand it. I told her of God's love for her and our family. She told me she'd been praying, asking for Heavenly Father to bring her comfort. That night I recognized for the first time, the influence for good our Baby Kevin was already having in our lives.

11

Baby Kevin's Song

I have four wonderful sisters who checked in on me often and rallied around me in their own special ways. Kimmy, my only sister living nearby at the time, brought me, on more than one occasion, her homemade sour cream lemon pie. I never appreciated comfort food as much as I did in those months. Tricia, who lives in Texas, read everything she could get her hands on about Trisomy 13 babies. She researched online about other Trisomy moms, sending me their stories and a few hopeful statistics. My youngest sister Megan had just moved from Utah to Boston. She hated being so far away and encouraged me to come visit for a few days, which I did when I was about 24 weeks pregnant. Tricia and our sister-in-law Mindy joined us. It was a wonderful vacation and just what I needed. Before going to Boston I had been hesitant to leave the safety I felt at home with Kevin and the kids.

I had many tender mercies throughout the trip; little signs from God letting me know he was near. One experience I'll never forget was waiting for a train in the subway. We rode the subway several times each day and there were almost always musicians performing...a man playing a harmonica, another man playing the guitar and singing, a woman playing a harp, etc. We usually only had a minute or two wait for our trains, except for this one particular time. I think we waited around 10 minutes and all the while there was a man playing a mandolin. He played various hymns and it was so beautiful. As he began to play "Be Still My Soul," a peace washed over me and it was like Jesus was right there with me in the subway. Those days in Boston helped me see how important it was that I keep living and experiencing life.

My sister Natalie lives in the Seattle area and of all my sisters, she could most relate to what I was going through. Her seven year old daughter, EmmaLee, had been born with a serious heart condition and had emergency open heart surgery when she was just a few days old. She was later diagnosed with DiGeorge Syndrome, a disorder caused by a defect in chromosome 22. Natalie would write me emails offering comfort and sharing her experiences with EmmaLee. In one email she suggested we choose a song for Baby Kevin. She'd had a song she sang to EmmaLee while she was pregnant and continued to sing it to her while she was in the NICU. EmmaLee loved the song and it was a source of comfort to her and my sister.

I liked the idea of choosing a song for Baby Kevin and made a mental note to talk to the family about it during dinner later that night. I went on with my day, and as I was in the bathroom blow drying my hair, "The Church of Jesus Christ," lyrics popped into my head and I realized I'd been singing it to myself quite often the past few days, which was a little strange because it wasn't a song our family had ever sang together in our family worship nights. It was one of the newer children's songs in our church and the only time I'd heard it was the few times I'd worked with the children in our Sunday meetings. I didn't even know the exact name of the song, but somehow, I remembered the words. I knew right then, "*The Church of Jesus Christ*," was his song. I shared it with the family later that night and it became our Baby Kevin's Song.

"I belong to The Church of Jesus Christ of Latter-Day Saints. I know who I am, I know God's plan, I'll follow him in faith. I believe in the Savior Jesus Christ, I'll honor his name. I'll do what is right, I'll follow his light. His truth I will proclaim."

Every time I thought of the words I would think of our family, and how this song described our testimony of Christ and our faith in God's plan for our baby. The song brought me a great deal of comfort. One day as I was driving Dakota to the orthodontist and thinking about Baby Kevin's song, I had the overwhelming feeling that this song was about how our Baby Kevin felt. It was his testimony of Jesus; he knew God's plan for him, and he was following Christ in faith. In that moment I had no doubt that he was a strong and faithful spirit.

BECKY BECK

12

Believe

I believe God is aware of each of us. He knows
our past, present and future. I have no doubt
he was aware of me during my pregnancy and the
months that followed. Believe was a recurring theme
throughout my pregnancy. It first surfaced the day I
received the phone call from Fetal Fotos. On my porch
that same morning a small gift bag was left for me
from some of the women in my church. Inside was
a bracelet with tiny beads spelling the word *Believe*.
Then later that night I was looking for a scripture
to share in our family worship night. I opened the
Bible, and when I looked down, my eyes went right
to Christ's words in Mark chapter 5 verse 36 and I felt
my Savior speak so clear to me, "Be not afraid, only

believe." Two simple assurances that while I didn't know what was coming, God did.

During my trip to Boston we visited Mindy's friends in the Cape Cod area. I was having a rough day. I felt so unsettled. My mind was filled with worry and concern for the baby. I had spent some time after church talking with the mother of a special needs baby and found myself questioning my own ability to care for a special needs child if Baby Kevin were to live.

After church we stopped at a home Mindy's friends were looking to buy. Their realtor let us have a tour of the house. It was a beautiful home with lots of charm and character. After our tour we waited for Mindy's friends in the foyer. My sisters were visiting, but I was in my own little world. I felt as if I were in a fog. I was tired emotionally and physically and ready to get off my feet, when I happened to glance down. There, sitting on the bookshelf was a little metal sign that said *Believe*. It was all I could do not to burst into tears. I knew it was another message from the Lord, reminding me He was aware of what I was going through and that everything would be ok. The spirit of Christ spoke these things directly to my heart and my unsettled feelings were replaced with peace.

Later in my pregnancy I read about a mother who was also expecting a Trisomy 13 little boy. She mentioned that rather than preparing for death, she found solace in preparing for life. She made sure her baby had all the things a newborn would need and even set up a nursery. At that particular stage of my pregnancy, I wasn't doing much of anything to prepare for life. I wasn't preparing for death either. I was in limbo. I decided to follow this mother's example and prepare for life.

The next morning as Janie, our 4 year old got out of the shower, I wrapped her in her towel--a bath towel my friend Amy made for her when she was born. Janie loved it and right then I decided to make one for Baby Kevin. I was already planning to go to Walmart that day, so I added *towels* to my list. I needed a full size bath towel and a smaller hand towel to make the hood. Just thinking about going shopping for the supplies made me happy.

Later, as I walked slowly down the towel aisle looking for something fun for a boy, I saw a bright green towel with a little frog on it and I knew that was the one. I glanced to the left of the froggie towel and folded right beside it was a towel with the word *Believe* on it. I just stared and almost gasped right out loud when I saw it. So, there I stood, in the towel aisle at Walmart, my heart about to burst, feeling so much love from my Father in Heaven. I was reminded once again that He was in charge, He was aware of me and that somehow everything would be okay.

13

Searching for Answers

Our family are members of The Church of Jesus Christ of Latter-Day Saints. Christ is at the head of our church, and he has called prophets and apostles to lead and guide us, just as he did in his ministry on earth. In our faith, when we marry in one of God's holy temples, we are sealed as husband and wife for eternity. "Until death do we part," is not a part of the ceremony. We are sealed to our spouse and to Christ forever. The sealing also applies to our children. We believe that if our spouse or one of our children pass away, through the sealing power of God, we will be with them again in heaven when we die. When Christ returns to the earth at His Second Coming, we will all be resurrected and our spirits will reunite with our bodies and we will be able to be with our families again here on earth. Whether on earth or in heaven, we will always be a family.

We have learned through scripture and living prophets that any children who may have died in infancy or childhood will be returned to us the same age they were when they died, and we will be able to raise them. I believe with all my heart that one day I will hold my Baby Kevin, healed of all his infirmities through Christ, and together Kevin and I will be able to raise him. God is a just and loving God and will one day make up for all our losses.

When we were told at 20 weeks that our baby could die in utero, it raised some questions. If our son was stillborn, did he have a spirit, and would he be ours in the next life? Or, was he simply a body growing inside me? Kevin was especially concerned and began searching the scriptures and the words of our living prophets. The information we found confirmed our hopes that even if our son died before birth, he would still be ours in the next life and we would have the privilege of raising him. These quotes by the prophet

Joseph Smith, who lost several children of his own, bring me great comfort.

"A question may be asked— 'Will mothers have their children in eternity?' Yes! Yes! Mothers, you shall have your children; for they shall have eternal life, for their debt is paid."

"Children ... must rise just as they died; we can there hail our lovely infants with the same glory—the same loveliness in the celestial glory."[1]

And one of my favorite scriptures in Hebrew chapter 11 verse 35 reads, "Women recieved their dead raised to life again."

---

1. 1.Smith, Joseph.

https://www.lds.org/manual/teachings-joseph-smith/chapter-14?lang=eng#7- 36481_000_018

14

Hope

I like Wikipedia's description of the word hope. "Hope is an optimistic attitude of mind that is based on an expectation of positive outcomes related to events and circumstances in one's life." After receiving our fatal diagnosis, hope was the one thing I clung to every day of my pregnancy. Hope for healing, hope for a misdiagnosis, and most of all, hope for a miracle. I always looked forward to my doctor visits and ultrasounds. I went into every appointment with my heart filled to the brim with hope that somehow there would be some sort of improvement.

I remember during one of my ultrasounds, the technician kept listing off all of the problems she was seeing. I finally stopped her and asked if she'd please tell me what looked right with our baby. The only thing she could say was that his spine looked good. Despite the feelings of despair I felt after most of my doctor appointments, I still managed to work through my grief and revisit my safe place of hope. Some might have called it denial, but I didn't care. Hope kept me sane, hope kept me from falling apart, and hope gave me the courage to face whatever was coming.

I remember scouring the internet for any stories of miracles relating to Trisomy 13 babies. I not only hoped for my own miracle, I had complete faith that Christ could give us one. While the ideal would have been giving birth to a perfectly healed baby, I knew the more practical miracle would be that his heart and brain weren't as bad as they looked on the ultrasounds, that his clefts could be fixed, and while he would certainly have his challenges, he would live. We would love him completely and he could have a happy life, despite any physical and mental limitations. I think Kevin knew from the start that what we were seeing on the ultrasounds was accurate. He walked the fine line of trying to help me realize the reality of our baby's condition, while at the same time respecting and supporting my need to have hope. I'll forever be grateful to him for that.

In the third chapter of Daniel in the Old Testament we see the courage of the three young Israelites, Shadrach, Meshach, and Abed-nego quietly refusing King Nebuchadnezzar's demand to worship his golden idol. The king informed the young men that if they did not fall down before the golden image, "...ye shall be cast the same hour into the midst of a burning fiery furnace." And then the king asked, "And who is that God that shall deliver you out of my hands?" Shadrach, Meshach, and Abed-nego responded without hesitation, "If it be so, (that you threaten us with death) our God whom we serve is able to deliver us from the burning fiery furnace...But if not (if for whatever reason He chooses not to save us from the fire), be it known unto thee, O King, that we will not serve thy gods, nor worship the golden image which thou hast set up." (KJV, Daniel 3:17-18)

I love that story. I love the complete faith of Shadrach, Meshach and Abed-nego. They were loyal to their God and even if He chose not to save them from the fiery furnace, they trusted Him. As much as I hoped for a miracle, "But if not," I had complete faith in my Heavenly Father's plan for our son and I was willing to give him back, whenever God chose to take him.

15

Love Notes

I can honestly say that Baby Kevin's pregnancy was my favorite. The first 19 weeks I was blissfully ignorant that anything was wrong. Weeks 20-23 were the hardest, trying to wrap my mind around how serious his diagnosis was and dealing with the grief. Weeks 24-37, while still hard, were also really blessed. I let my faith in the Lord remove my fear and I didn't take one minute of having that baby inside me for granted. The love I felt for him and the love I felt from him is hard to explain, but so very sweet.

My prayers became more frequent and fervent. I remember one day, dropping to my knees in the laundry room and pouring my heart out to the Lord, begging for a miracle; but with open hands, ready to accept His will. The strength I felt from my Savior was my lifeline. I could literally feel him helping me to not only get through the pregnancy, but to see all the blessings surrounding me. I enjoyed taking care of my home and family, carrying out my church responsibilities, and just living life. Woven thickly between the moments of sadness, I experienced a great deal of gratitude, peace and joy every day.

The week leading up to Baby Kevin's birth was a challenging one. I prefer dealing with one tough thing at a time, but that isn't always the way things go. More often than not, there's a handful of hard things going on at once, and that week was no exception. I was torn between being ready to give birth, and wanting to keep Baby Kevin safe inside me forever. I continued to pray for a miracle, but also knew the worst case scenario was possible. A few days before our son was born, three of the companies who were renting property from us changed their mind and decided not to renew their leases. It was too late in the year to find other companies to replace them, which meant a huge pay cut for our family. The city also came in and threatened to shut down part of our business if we didn't make some changes to our property.

I couldn't believe the timing of it all, but one good thing happened the day before the birth. I had the thought to write each of the kids a love note to put in their lunches for the following day. I expressed my love for each of them and assured them all would be well. Focusing on the love I felt for my children was a much needed distraction and seemed to melt away all the frustration of the week.

16

Baby Kevin's Birth Day

I was scheduled to be induced the morning of Thursday, May 10th, 2012. I got about four hours of sleep before waking up at 5:00 a.m. I said a heartfelt prayer, and then took a shower. I'd been so tired throughout the week that I hadn't showered since Sunday. I couldn't remember the last time I'd gone so long between showers. I wanted our family to begin the day as normal as possible, so we had our usual morning routine of family scripture study and prayer before breakfast.

We traded cars with my parents the night before so my mom could use our suburban to pick up all the kids from school. When we went out to the van that morning to leave for the hospital, the battery was dead. After the week we'd had we weren't the least bit surprised and joked that we would have been more surprised if it had started.

We checked into Labor & Delivery at the University of Utah Hospital. I changed into one of the new cute hospital gowns I'd brought. The nurse hooked me up to the antibiotic for strep B, and against my better judgement, Pitocin (I hadn't needed Pitocin with most of my babies). The antibiotic took two hours to be released into my system and then another two hours to take effect. Kev and I passed the time reading well wishes on Facebook and Kevin read the book Unbroken to me. As the minutes ticked by, my contractions started getting really uncomfortable. I asked the nurse to check me, but she put me off for half an hour. When I arrived at the hospital around 7:30 a.m. I was dilated at a three+, then at noon when they finally checked me, I was at an eight. Five minutes later, a nine.

At that point I knew it was too late for an epidural. I was so angry with the nurses for not listening to me when I told them I didn't need Pitocin. I finally demanded that they shut it off. We had no cell service and the land line wasn't working, so Kevin ran outside to call Heather, our birth photographer. I knew there was no way she could get there in time. She knew it too. The little bit of a plan we had for the timing of things went out the window. I felt frantic but also somehow calm at the thought of having the baby natural. Something inside me was telling me I could do it. I had about a two minute break between contractions (something I'd never had with Dakota's natural birth) and that helped me refocus. A wonderful nurse pushed on my knees just right, which really helped with the back pain and pressure. Kevin finally returned and I could hear him telling me over and over, "You have to breathe, Beck, you have to breathe." As I gripped the handles of the hospital bed through the contractions, I tried harder to focus on my breathing. I had my wits about me and felt somewhat in control, something I never felt during Dakota's birth, so I was grateful for that.

Two pushes and he was born. Kevin David Beck Jr entered the world at 12:26 p.m. and he was alive. The doctor knew immediately that he did, in fact, have Trisomy 13. The moment I saw him, I knew it too. His facial features were clear indicators. Not all Trisomy 13 babies are strong enough to cry, but Baby Kevin cried. He cried for at least 10 minutes as I held him close. I'm so grateful Kevin thought to record some of it. It was the sweetest little cry, and so helpless. I kept trying to quiet him, but I don't think he wanted to be quieted. I think he was letting us all know he'd made it, and I wonder if he wasn't just as sad to leave us, as we were to let him go. While I wasn't surprised to see his diagnosis confirmed, I was incredibly sad to see how sick he was. I had faith that things would be better for him, right up to the minute he was born.

Jackson, my dad, and Kevin's dad arrived at the hospital in time to give Baby Kevin a name and a blessing. Kevin gave our son a beautiful blessing. While receiving his name and blessing was not a saving ordinance, it was special to us for Kevin to be able to bless our son. We didn't have him baptized because our faith teaches that baptism isn't necessary for children under eight, as they are all saved through Christ. In the New Testament Jesus taught that little children are inherently good and pure. The Book of Mormon, Another Testament of Jesus Christ, teaches in Moroni chapter 8 verse 8, "little children are whole, for they are not capable of committing sin." And in verse 12 of that same chapter we are taught, "little children are alive in Christ, even from the foundation of the world."

Jackson brought a little hat he'd crocheted for Baby Kevin in one of his art classes at school. He was the only one of our children who got to hold his brother while he was still alive. It was sweet to witness him love on his little brother and participate in his blessing.

My mom scrambled to pick up all the kids from their three different schools. Had we known things would progress so quickly we would have brought them up sooner. I was worried about how they would react to their brother's face, I thought maybe if he had a bath and I dressed him in his baby clothes, it might help.

I was pretty sure he was still breathing, barely, when I handed him over to the nurse for his bath, but it was hard to tell. I worried he passed away at some point during the bath because when the nurse returned him to me, he felt different. I was heartbroken. What in the world was I thinking letting the nurse bathe him? Of course that would be too much for him to handle. But I wasn't thinking, I was in some strange place in my head I'd never been before. I wanted to do all the right things, but wasn't sure what those things were.

We checked for a heartbeat, but there was none. I was devastated. Our guess is that he lived just over an hour. Shortly after he passed, the rest of the kids arrived. Some with tear-stained faces, but all of them excited to meet their little brother. It was hard to watch them get more and more emotional as time went on, but they loved being able to hold him. They didn't care how he looked or what he was wearing. They just loved him with their whole hearts. Heather Nann, our photographer, arrived shortly before the kids and captured so many beautiful moments. I am so grateful I thought to hire a birth photographer. I did some research to find one who I felt comfortable sharing such a sacred event with. Heather was so respectful and most of the time I didn't even notice she was there.

Kevin asked my dad to offer a family prayer. In addition to our children and our fathers, my best friend Marci, our mothers, and Kevin's brother and sister were there as well. Dad gave a beautiful prayer. We felt heaven near in that hospital room and I've wondered if there weren't angels there too—family members from heaven, supporting and comforting us.

After the prayer we brought out the birthday cake we had for Baby Kevin. It had 10 candles, one for each member of our family. It was nap time for Janie and she had been struggling, but she perked right up when she saw the candles. After several attempts to light them, Marci pulled out a nail file and that did the trick. We sang happy birthday and Kevin cut the cake. Later, we gathered around my hospital bed for family pictures. Me in my pink polka-dot hospital gown. The babies with bed heads from being woken up from their naps. And puffy faces from crying. None of that mattered though. Our baby had made it, and the few minutes we'd all had together were priceless.

After things settled down and everyone went home, Kevin and I had time to talk as we took turns holding our son. It was one of many bitter-sweet moments of that day. It was hard knowing it was only his body with us, but a comfort knowing his spirit was alive and well, he was just too perfect for this life. As I held my little Kevin with both of us snuggled up to my big Kevin, it seemed to get harder the longer we had him, so around 8:30 p.m. we sent him to the morgue.

Kevin and I talked through our feelings. I wrestled with regret over not being able to talk to Baby Kevin while he was alive. There were things I wanted to tell him, but there was so much going on and always other people around. Kevin was feeling guilt, like somehow losing our son was his fault. I felt so bad about that, as he had nothing to feel guilty about. I worried about Kevin. All his energy was focused on me and the kids, and making sure we were okay. I was the center of all the support from family and friends. Kevin was our rock, and I wondered if he was getting the support he needed.

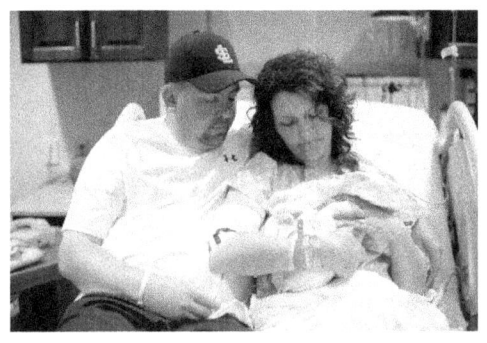

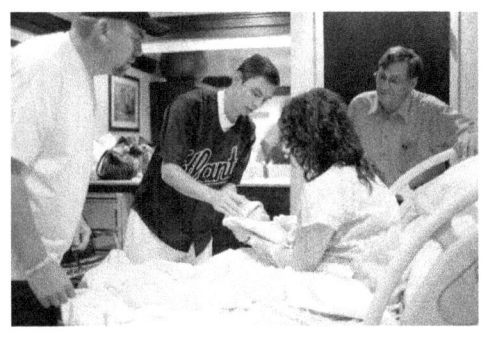

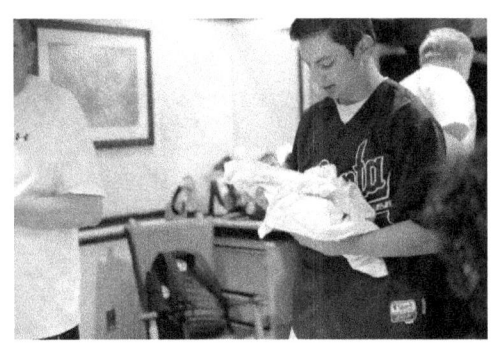

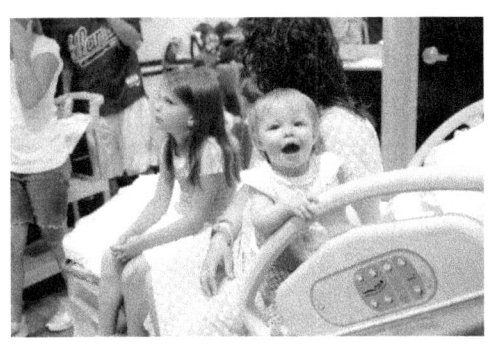

BECKY BECK

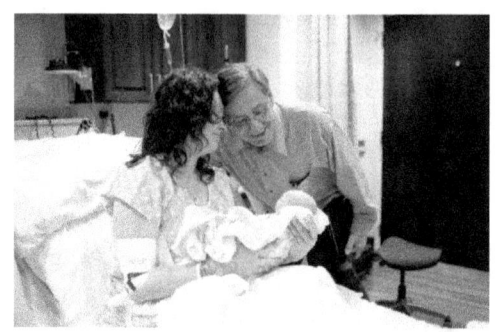

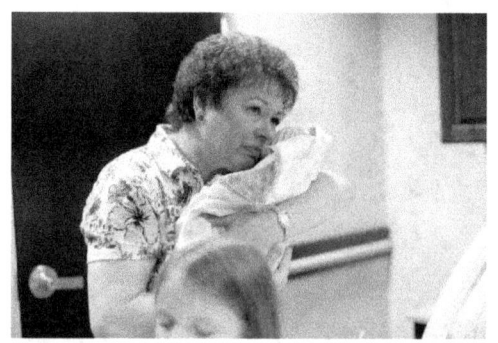

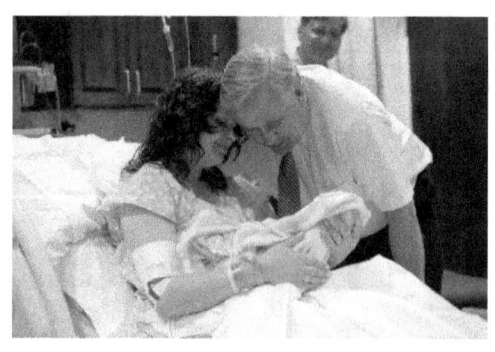

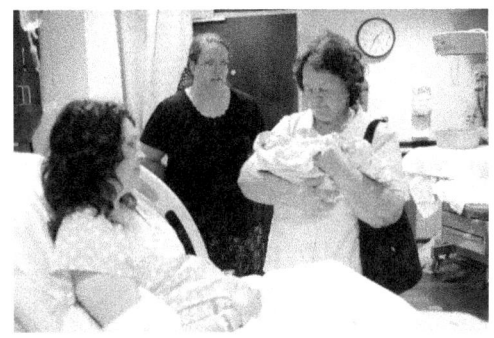

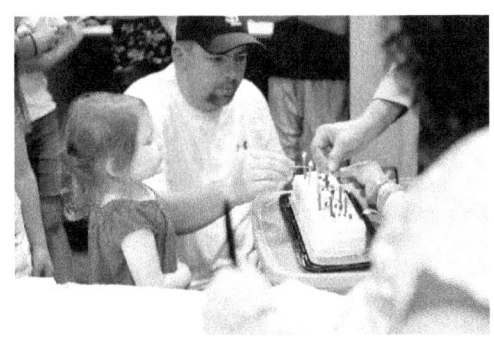

17

Going Home Empty Handed

We left the hospital around noon the following day. I couldn't wait to get out of there. I'd only slept about three hours since the birth and I just wanted to be home. We drove up to the house and were greeted by the big pots on our porch filled with freshly planted flowers. We later found out Kevin's family had planted them while we were at the hospital. Everyone was surprised to see us, they assumed we'd be staying another night. Coming home empty handed was strange and painful, but I was so grateful I had two babies to come home to and I couldn't help but feel so grateful God had given me my two little "extra" girls.

I dealt with waves of emotion all day. Kevin took the kids to his parents' house for dinner, so I had some time alone. As soon as they left I completely fell apart. I sobbed harder than I ever had before. The sorrow I felt was nothing like I'd ever experienced. I cried until there were no tears left. I was completely worn out and tired so I took some melatonin and slept hard from 9:30 p.m. to 1:30 a.m. I woke up to a dark and quiet house. I got up and as I rounded the corner into our living room I spotted a little gift box waiting for me on our piano. It was from my brother Rick and his wife Mindy. Inside was a beautiful emerald pendant necklace. I began to cry as I realized it was Baby Kevin's birth stone. Such a thoughtful gift.

I couldn't go back to sleep, so I read through a family Facebook feed I'd started with my parents and siblings when we got to the hospital. That was how we kept them updated, since we didn't have cell phone service. I read the messages between my brothers and sisters going back and forth, wondering how I was doing, talking about random funny things, and then discussing airfare and arrival times after finding out Baby Kevin didn't make it. I am so grateful for the relationship I have with them. They all flew in for the graveside service, coming from Seattle, Arizona, Texas and Boston. They also covered the cost of the casket and headstone and my parents covered the cost of the burial. We were incredibly grateful not to have to worry about any of those expenses.

In the days that followed, the doorbell just kept ringing with friends and family dropping off food and gifts. So much love was showered upon our family. I remember thinking I was going to need a case of thank you cards, when not long after the door bell rang and my friend Debbie had left a box of thank you note cards on my porch.

In the days that followed I spent hours in my recliner icing my breasts, trying to encourage my milk to dry up. I'd also read that cold cabbage leaves would help. They were a lifesaver. I remember the night my milk came in. I'd fallen asleep watching the latest Mission Impossible with the family and woke up with chills worse than I'd ever experienced. My milk was coming in and I couldn't stop shaking. Kevin got me in bed, covered me with several blankets and then laid right on top of me, trying to help me get me warm.

The shaking finally slowed and then the tears started to flow. I was so emotional. One minute I was fine and the next I wasn't. I had no idea how much losing my baby would hurt.

I woke up the next morning, Mother's Day, to Janie snuggling in bed with us. I heard her tell her Daddy, "Jesus is going to fix Baby Kevin's lip," (he did in fact have a double cleft lip and palate). I knew she was right. He would fix his lip, his heart, his brain, and every other chromosome in his body that wasn't right. I love the scripture in The Book of Mormon, Another Testament of Jesus Christ where we're taught in Alma chapter 40 verse 23. "The soul shall be restored to the body, and the body to the soul; yea, and every limb and joint shall be restored to its body; yea, even a hair of the head shall not be lost; but all things shall be restored to their proper and perfect frame."

My boys came in to wish me a happy Mother's Day and give me a hug. Kloe brought me breakfast and they all took care of me the rest of the day. Kevin's family stopped by. His brother and sister gave me a beautiful necklace. My brother-in-law made me a strawberry pie and my mother-in-law made me the most beautiful minky blanket which I love and still treasure. The hospital had several molds made of Baby Kevin's hands and feet, so we gave one to each of our moms for Mother's Day. I loved those molds and everything else that reminded me he lived: his birth certificate, his social security card, and all the pictures.

Kevin made a delicious steak dinner that night, and as we gathered around the dining room table we talked about Baby Kevin's graveside service. We decided to write letters to Baby Kevin and put them in the balloons we'd release during the service. That way if there were things we wanted to say to him, but weren't able to in the hospital, we could write them in our letters. We invited the entire extended family to participate.

18

The Mortuary

The days following Baby Kevin's death are a blur. My family arrived one by one throughout the week and it was so great to see them. Tricia and Natalie helped me with the and spent time just sitting and talking with me. Time seemed to slow down just a little that week and I slowly felt my strength returning.

I remember one night everyone was writing their letters to Baby Kevin, but I couldn't write mine. I struggled to put my feelings on paper. It was after 11:00 p.m. when I got ready for bed and in my prayers I asked for help. I got up from my knees, sat down and began to type. My thoughts and feelings came together, and the tears fell as I read and re-read the words I wanted to share with my son.

One morning was spent at the mortuary picking out a casket and dressing Baby Kevin for his burial. My sisters Tricia, Natalie, and Kim came with me. There were only two caskets to choose from, so the choice was easy. I went with the simple white one that had two handles so my boys could carry it. I thought I was doing a pretty good job of keeping my emotions in check, but as I looked at those tiny caskets, I broke down. My sisters hugged me, and we all cried together.

Next, I was able to dress my baby. I was so happy to see him, and he really looked so good. He was only wearing a diaper and his cheeks were pink and the swelling in his face had gone down. It was the first time he and I were alone together. I loved dressing him and holding him. I told him how much I loved him and how grateful I was to be his mama. I thanked him for his life and for the way he'd blessed me and our family. It was very healing to have that quiet time with him after feeling as though things were so crazy and rushed in the hospital.

When we were finished, I invited my sisters in to see and hold Baby Kevin. They all loved on him through their tears. It didn't cross my mind until then that they would all want to meet him—I still wasn't thinking straight. Later in the day my parents, my sister Megan, and my brother Rick and his wife Mindy came to see him. Megan took pictures of everyone holding Baby Kevin and some of him in his casket. Such tender moments I will never forget.

It occurred to me while I was holding Baby Kevin in the mortuary that I'd never gotten to rock him. I wished so badly the mortuary had a rocker. I'd spent hours and hours rocking all my babies, it was one of my favorite things to do. A couple of months later our family and my cousin Mike's family donated a rocker to the mortuary. Two days after Baby Kevin died they lost their 14 year old son due to a heart attack. Shortly after we made the donation my friend Elise was able to hold and rock her angel baby, who had Trisomy 18, in the rocking chair we'd donated. Every time I see our friends who work at the mortuary, they express their thanks and tell me what a blessing the rocker has been for so many.

I went home from the mortuary emotionally and physically exhausted. Kevin wanted his last memories to be of kissing his son's soft little cheeks in the hospital, so he didn't go to the mortuary. I buried my head in his chest and cried as I told him how wonderful it was to hold our baby again.

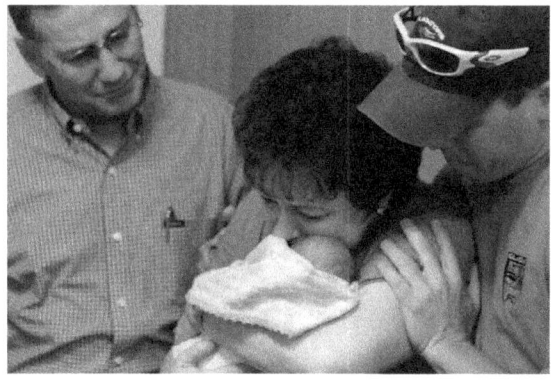

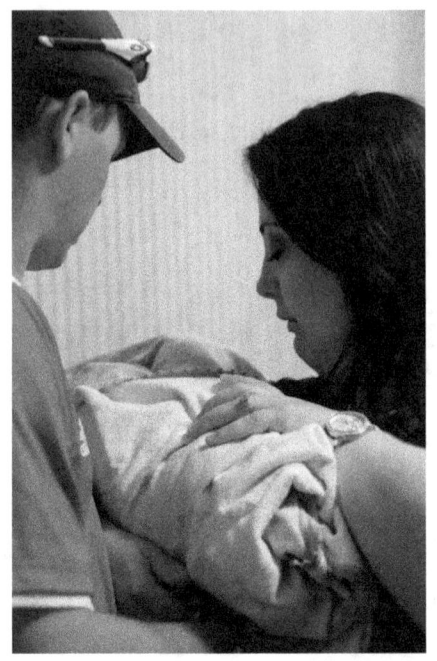

19

The Graveside and a Letter

We buried Baby Kevin on Saturday, May 19th, 2012. When we got up that morning the balloons we'd filled with helium and our letters to Baby Kevin the night before, were all laying on the ground. I didn't know what to do. The balloon launch was an important part of the graveside. Kevin's dad suggested we pop the balloons and put the letters in an envelope inside the casket, so that's what we did. Kevin made a quick trip to the store and bought a helium tank and more balloons to fill once we arrived at the cemetery.

We pulled into the mortuary parking lot at 9:00 a.m. I was going to see Baby Kevin one more time while my brother Rob and brother-in-law Scott met him.

Daren, our family friend and the funeral director, would seal the casket when we were finished. The night before, when we'd discussed how the morning would go, Kevin and the kids didn't think they wanted to see Baby Kevin again. However, when we arrived at the mortuary Kevin told them, "If anyone would like to see Baby Kevin one more time, this is your last chance." I went in first and when I glanced behind me, they were all there following me. I was so happy they'd changed their minds.

Everyone had an opportunity to hold Baby Kevin again, including my dad. After my brothers and dad left, Kevin gave a family prayer. It was a beautiful moment, with our entire family gathered in prayer. We took one more family picture. No planning went into that photo--a few of the girls were still wearing the curlers they'd worn to bed, and Lilly was wearing her pajamas, but it didn't matter. We put the letters and a fishing lure (our family loves to fish) in the casket, but then I was horrified at the possibility of one of the hooks poking him. We ended up covering each hook with the plastic backs to my earrings. They worked perfectly. Daren sealed the casket, and my boys carried their brother to our car.

When my Grandpa Moon learned of our baby's diagnosis months earlier, he offered the other half of his son Boyd's grave, who died as an infant. He was buried in Malad, Idaho, about two hours north of our home in Salt Lake. My mom was raised there, and I was born there. Initially I'd thought I wanted him buried closer to our home, but as time passed, I knew Malad was the right place where he would be surrounded by many family members who I loved.

I think one of the things I appreciated most about this day was that nothing was rushed. We kept the service small, inviting only our immediate families, Marci, and Grandpa Moon. When everyone arrived we took pictures, since I knew I'd be in no mood to do it after the service. Our boys looked so handsome carrying their brother from the car to the grave. Kevin's dad conducted, and we began by singing How Firm a Foundation followed by a beautiful opening prayer given by Kevin's brother Steve. Emmy shared a scripture she chose from The Book of Mormon, Another Testament of Jesus Christ in the book of

Mosiah chapter 4 verse 9, "Believe in God; believe that he is, and that he created all things, both in heaven and in earth; believe that he has all wisdom, and all power, both in heaven and in earth; believe that man doth not comprehend all the things which the Lord can comprehend."

Then I shared my letter to Baby Kevin...

My Dear Sweet Baby Kevin, You and I have quite the history together! I've been looking forward to your arrival for almost 8 years. I had no idea how long it would take to get you here, the amount of girls who needed to come before you, or how hard you'd have to fight to make it to our family. Your time on earth was so short. I wanted to tell you so many things that I wasn't able to. I wanted to tell you how much I love you, how grateful I am to be your mother, and how thankful I am for all you've given me over the years. You've blessed my life in so many ways. Because of you, my faith in and understanding of our Savior's Atonement has grown. My testimony of prayer and personal revelation has been strengthened. Because of you, I've seen the hand of the Lord in my life and the life of our family.

Because of you, I've seen the Christ-like love of others who have reached out to comfort, support and encourage our family. Because of you, our family is stronger, and our faith is firm in our Heavenly Father's plan. Because of you, I appreciate each one of your brothers and sisters more, and I try every day to be a better wife and mother.

I had hoped to have had a little more time to get to know you. But as I've thought about it, I learned quite a bit about you during the months you were growing inside me. I remember driving with Dakota to the orthodontist one day. I was singing the words to your song in my head. When I would sing your song, I usually pictured our family singing it to you, but this particular day you let me know that this song was your song because it was your testimony. You know You belong to The Church of Jesus Christ of Latter Day Saints, You know who you are, You know God's plan, and You are following Him in Faith. You believe in your Savior Jesus Christ, You honor His name. You do what is right, You follow his light, His truth You will proclaim. I knew that day, the spirit inside me, your spirit, was incredibly strong and faithful and that you had a special purpose to fulfill.

Another thing I learned about you is that you were concerned about me. You always wanted me to know you were okay. You were the most active baby of all your brothers and sisters. Any time I would wonder if you were alright, within seconds of the thought, I'd feel a kick or some other movement letting me know you were alive and well.

I learned you were determined and strong-willed. You most definitely were determined to come to earth and get a body. It is a miracle you made it full term, given all your physical challenges. You are a fighter and I thank you for fighting so hard to be born into our family. I think about how hard and how long you cried shortly after you were born. I kept talking to you, trying to calm you down, but as I think back on it now, I have no doubt you didn't want to be quieted. You wanted everyone to know you made it, and oh the things you could have told us if only you were able to talk!

I need to thank you for blessing the lives of your brothers and sisters. Last Fall I remember offering a heartfelt prayer to my Heavenly Father. I asked that my children might come to know their Savior while they were young so that they'd know they could turn to Him for help when they needed it. It was just a few months later that we learned of all your physical challenges. Our journey with you has been an answer to that prayer as I've watched each member of our family grow closer to Jesus Christ.

I want you to know how much I love your Daddy. I was so happy when he told me he'd like to give you his name. Your Daddy is a good man who loves the Lord, honors his priesthood and takes such good care of our family. You are also named after your Grandpa Dave. He too is a wonderful man who you can be proud to be named after. Heavenly Father has been so good to me. He's blessed me with the gospel of Jesus Christ in my life and a wonderful family. He blessed me with you and although I had to give you back to Him for now, know that I look forward to raising you one day. I'll miss you and I'll think about you every day until then.

I love you, Mom

I considered having Kevin read the letter, because I wasn't sure I could do it. But I wanted to be the one to say those words to my boy, and I got through it. After I finished, Jackson dedicated the grave. It was the sweetest, most heartfelt prayer I have ever heard. When he finished, he was sobbing and he hugged and hugged Kevin and me. He was so overcome with emotion. Dakota was sobbing as well. They were both so excited to have another brother. All the kids were. As hard as it was to watch our children grieve, we knew it was good for them to experience those emotions and not hold it all in.

Mindy brought a basket full of Kleenex packets, and I think everyone went through at least one of them. I was so grateful my Grandpa Moon could be there. He stood by me throughout the entire service. He'll never know how thankful we are to him for giving us the grave site. My Grandma Moon is buried right next to Baby Kevin and one day Grandpa Moon will be buried there too. It is such a beautiful little cemetery and it makes me happy to think of him there.

After Jackson dedicated the grave, Emmy, Kloe, Gracie and my niece Kaitlynn played Baby Kevin's song on their violins with my sister Kimmy accompanying them on the keyboard. It was perfect. Towards the end we all sang along with them. Kevin's dad said a few words, and then my brother Rob gave the closing prayer. We passed the balloons around and it was a beautiful thing to watch the blue, light blue and white balloons fill the sky.

Everyone left for the restaurant except our little family. We took a few minutes to share our feelings. Kloe told us how all of this had helped her appreciate her brothers and sisters more. Kevin talked about how important it is that we all work to be better so we can be with Baby Kevin one day. I told them how much I loved each of them. The boys went over to the casket one more time. Jackson lingered to say a few words and I watched the tears fall down his cheeks as he spoke to his brother.

We joined the others at The Dude Ranch in Malad for lunch. Everyone was starving after such an emotional afternoon. They serve all sorts of comfort food and it was just what we all needed. We decided that day, we would start a tradition of going to The Dude Ranch every time we went to visit the grave.

BECKY BECK

20

Driving Away

As I gazed at the cemetery from the freeway on our way home, the tears started to fall. My heart was full of both sadness and gratitude. Sadness at the thought of not seeing or holding my baby again, for what felt like such a long time. Gratitude because I knew I would see him again. I would on day be able to hold him, rock him, and love on him. We'd pick up right where we left off, except my sick baby would be perfect. I felt gratitude for the incredible faith- building experience this baby had brought to our family, and I was so thankful for his beautiful, peaceful resting place.

By the time we got home, we were all completely exhausted. Poor Lilly was running a fever and fussed for most of the drive. She'd missed her nap, been in the sun too long, and was teething. But even that was a blessing, as I was able to turn my focus to her and concentrate on being her mom and meeting her needs. She was the most wonderful distraction and comfort that day, and continued to be in the days and months that followed.

I thought I'd feel some sort of relief after the graveside service, but I only felt sad and empty. My baby was buried. I'd taken care of all his earthly needs. There was nothing more to do; it was over. The sadness I felt was all-consuming, but I learned that if I could take it one day at a time, sometimes just one moment at a time, I could get through. I continued to grieve and mourn in my own way, but my grief ran parallel to all the other good things going on in my life. I never tried to avoid or block out the grief. I allowed myself to feel all of it, but careful not to lose myself in it. I have come to learn that it's okay to be sad, to grieve and to mourn. Sadness can be a blessing because it reminds us of the people and relationships in our lives that really matter.

As I continued to look to my Savior for strength, he blessed me, carried me, and helped me see and experience all the good that continued to surround me. I worked hard at living in the present and that made all the difference.

Even now, all these years later, I still experience waves of sadness here and there. I've come to welcome those feelings as reminders. Reminders of my son and the way he blessed my life during those months I was privileged to carry him, reminders of the way he continues to bless our family, and reminders of all the good things today and good things to come.

113

Epilogue

Life Goes On

O ver 10 years have passed since we said goodbye to our son and brother. Kevin and I will celebrate 30 years of marriage this year and our family continues to grow. I have become a grief coach, helping other grieving mamas navigate through their grief journey. Kevin is retired and spends much of his time with church service, taking care of his wife and children's every need and creating videos for his Sluffin' It Outdoors YouTube channel. He's also written, Bones and the Treasure Map, a fun mystery/historical fiction book and audiobook based on some of our family's adventures.

Jackson married Aubrey and they have three sons, Beau, Logan and Will. They live in Mesa, Arizona where Jackson works as a Certified Financial Planner with Taurum Retirement Partners and Aubrey is a freelance writer.

Emmy and her husband Garren and their daughter Maisie live in Herriman, Utah. Garren is a seminary teacher and Emmy is an accountant for the Utah Jazz.

Dakota and his wife Jenna recently graduated from Weber State University and also live in Herriman, Utah. Dakota is the Finance Manager for Grandcare and Jenna is an oncology nurse.

Kloe recently returned from her 18 month mission for The Church of Jesus Christ of Latter Day Saints in Paris, France, and is attending college at Southern Utah University.

Gracie graduates from high school this year and is preparing to serve a mission and attend college at Utah State University.

Janie is in the 8th grade and plays soccer and volleyball for her school.

Lilly is a 6th grader and loves being involved with the school Drama Company and rearranging her room weekly.

We love gathering for family dinners, heading to the mountains to fish, hunt, and camp, and taking sunny vacations together as often as we can.

Baby Kevin continues to be very much a part of our family. We feel him near in unique and special ways. Each time we visit the cemetery to celebrate his birthday and Christmas, we gather in a circle around his grave, hold hands as we sing his song, and have a family prayer thanking the Lord for Baby Kevin and all our many blessings. Then we head into town for a meal at the Dude Ranch.

You can learn more about our Heavenly Father, Jesus Christ, the plan of salvation and life after death at

http://www.churchofjesuschrist.org

Afterword

One of the unique parts of our grief journey was our efforts to love and support each of our children as they processed the loss of their brother in their own unique and individual ways. We encouraged them to write letters to Baby Kevin a few days after he passed and then later, at various times, our five oldest children wrote about their perspective, feelings and some of the things they experienced along their personal grief journey. I've included their words here, along with a link to my daughter Emmy performing "A Thousand Years" on her cello, another song we associate with Baby Kevin, that has become very dear to our family.

Jackson

Jackson was 18 when his brother died. He and Aubrey were dating at the time. A year later they were both serving missions for The Church of Jesus Christ of Latter Day Saints—Jackson in Brazil and Aubrey in Ukraine. Aubrey wrote to Jackson with some questions about Baby Kevin. They gave me permission to include them in a blog post on May 11th, 2017:

Aubrey wrote to Jackson: "The tenth of May is fast approaching. I remember I spent the evening with you after Baby Kevin had made both his entrance and exit. I remember you told me that you never want to forget him, never want to forget the influence he had on your family. And so I hope that you will take some time to remember. Write it down and send it my way, if you need.

Jackson's response: "I'm glad you asked about Baby Kevin. I thought about him a lot Friday, but it will be nice to write it down. Here is what I remember from that day: I got a phone call after my last class to come to the hospital. I had to miss a baseball game but I wasn't too worried about it. Both my grandpas got there just after me and we were in a little rush to give him a name and a blessing because we didn't know how long he would live. So we circled up and right as my dad was about to start he broke down. It was the first time I'd ever seen him cry. Then grandpa Dave gave him a hug and started crying too. Hadn't seen him cry either. Then everyone was crying for a short moment, but then we got it together and blessed him. Then we just took our turns holding him. He was alive, but you could barely tell. He would just gasp for air every few minutes. It broke your heart. He died shortly later before any of the rest of the family came. I don't remember much of the rest of the day other than sitting in the waiting room with everyone while the grandparents had a few minutes of alone time with him and my mom. I remember going to your house and going on a walk. And very long hugs.

I remember not knowing how to feel. I knew that he was saved and it was not a bad thing at all, but it didn't feel right not to be sad. I still don't know how sad to be. I don't really know how to feel at all. I felt bad for my mom and dad. I was disappointed to not have another brother. I guess we are the only ones I can be sad for because he has his ticket to heaven. I suppose us being without him is the sad part. Which is selfish.

Then I remember being really nervous to dedicate the grave. Then when I did it I cried through the whole thing, my body went numb, and I don't remember a single thing I said. It was long though. I struggle with speaking by the Spirit when I give blessings, but I definitely didn't then. It was like the lights went off for me and the Spirit just used me as a mouth piece.

And now here we are today, having pizza and ice cream on the 10th of every month. I still have to fight the urge to want to feel sad about it. There is nothing to be sad about. I have an angel working for me on the other side."

BECKY BECK

Emmy

Emmy was 16 when Baby Kevin died. As a senior in high school she wrote this essay for her english class:

I figured out my mom was pregnant before she intended to tell the rest of my siblings and me. I should have been used to the idea of my mom having babies; this was her eighth child after all. For some reason, though, it shocked me. My youngest sister wasn't even ten months old yet. Eight kids. It took me quite a while to process that thought.

About a week later, on Christmas Eve, my parents decided to tell the rest of my brothers and sisters about the baby. I remember watching the different emotions cross my older brother's face. First confusion, then disbelief, followed by shock, and finally excitement. We were all excited. My parents told us we were finding out the gender of the baby that day too. Every single one of us was hoping for a boy. The girls outnumbered the boys in my family five to two, and after four girls in a row, we were more than ready for a boy.

The ultrasound technician had a hard time figuring out exactly what gender the baby was. She ended up sending us home with "about an 80% chance it's a boy". We thought it was a little odd, but it was Christmas Eve and we were just happy the word "girl" didn't come out of her mouth.

The day after Christmas we packed up and headed to Arizona to spend the week with my aunt and uncle. Little did we know that would be the only week during my mom's pregnancy filled with bliss. Ignorant bliss, but bliss just the same. During that week we didn't know that the doctor would call as soon as we got home from our trip and tell us that the baby's head was abnormally large and he wanted to do further tests. During that week we didn't know that our baby brother had countless problems with his little heart and brain. We didn't know he had a bilateral cleft palate and lip, or that hardly anything in his tiny body developed right. During that week we didn't know that our baby brother, whom we had been anticipating the arrival of for years now, would only live for an hour and a half.

The next five months were the hardest of my life. At first I didn't believe the doctors. Nothing was wrong with my baby brother; that was impossible. But when specialist after specialist confirmed that what they had told us was true, it became harder to deny it. My baby brother had Trisomy 13. Trisomy 13, I couldn't even pronounce it. They told us it was a miracle he had even made it to 20 weeks. They asked my parents if they wanted to "terminate" the baby, like my brother was some sort of object rather than a human being. Thankfully that was out of the question for my parents and they decided to continue with the pregnancy, even with the risk of miscarrying at any time.

Everybody I knew asked me constantly about my mom and the baby, especially at first when they didn't really know specifics. It was exhausting. Their intentions were good and their hearts were in the right place, but I hated it. I hated that feeling I got in the back of my throat any time anyone asked me about it. It took all I had to hold back the tears that inevitably came. I just wanted to be left alone. Thankfully only a couple of my close friends at school knew about the baby. School got my mind off of things. There was something about walking through the halls and being anonymous in a sea of my peers that was almost comforting. Nobody knew. Nobody asked.

I did not know the true meaning of hope until those few months leading up to the birth of Baby Kevin. Despite what the doctors told us, I hoped that somehow Baby Kevin would live, even if he had some special needs. I also hoped by some miracle he would be just fine. It sounds ridiculous now, to hope for something that impossible, but I was desperate. I just wanted my baby brother. I had a renewed hope and faith in the Atonement of Jesus Christ. I had always known that I would get to be with my family again someday, but the knowledge that I get to live with my brother again, and that his body will be perfect, became so much more precious to me. It was the hope that carried me through those last few months. I'm glad that I had that hope. It would have been so easy to dismiss him and give up on him because that was all I knew. There was only that first week that I didn't know he had so many problems. Almost the entire time I knew my mom was going to have a baby, I also knew the baby had almost no chance of living. I was able to allow myself to see him as my little brother, even if we knew he wasn't going to live for very long.

The day finally came. May 10, 2012. It was a day that I wanted to be over as soon as possible and a day I wished would never come all at the same time. When we got to the hospital, my dad sat me and my little brother and sisters down. He told us that my mom had delivered the baby, and he did in fact have Trisomy 13. He wasn't expected to live long. I couldn't remember ever seeing my dad so emotional. He was my dad: the big, strong protector. I hated seeing him so vulnerable.

I met my baby brother, Kevin David Beck Jr., about two hours after he was born. He was such a sweet little thing, and so tiny. I held him and rocked him and sang to him. He never made any noise when he was with me. His heartbeat was so quiet and irregular, we aren't quite sure when exactly he passed away. The little guy fought pretty hard to live as long as he did. My parents tell me he cried for a good 10 minutes after he was born, he wanted to make sure everyone knew he made it.

The tears started sometime before we got to the hospital room and never really stopped that day. When we came home from the hospital, I wasn't quite sure what to do. I wasn't ready to deal with the pain yet, nor did I know how. The only thing I could do was lie on my parents' bed and watch other people deal with their problems on TV. Anytime I thought about what had happened that day, the tears would come again. Friends and family tried to contact me and tell me how sorry they were. I ignored everything for the first couple of days. I didn't want to talk about it; I just wanted to be left alone.

About a week later we buried my baby brother. We buried him in a beautiful, quiet cemetery in Malad, Idaho. That is a day I'll never forget. I will never forget how heartbreaking it was to listen to my mom read a letter she wrote to Baby Kevin. I will never forget the look on my older brother's face as he blessed his little brother's grave. I had never seen anyone in so much pain. It hurt to see him so grief-stricken. Everyone was so incredibly sad and there was nothing I could do to fix it. That was the worst part. You can't just fix these things, only time can do that.

I'm not quite sure how I made it through those five months. The sadness and pain never seemed like it would end. A few times it felt like the grief would just swallow me whole. But eventually, I did heal. I never thought I'd be able to handle losing a brother. It is amazing what we are capable of being put through, and our ability to still come out on top. You never really know how strong you are until you are put in a situation where you have no other choice.

Dakota

Dakota wrote this eight years after Baby Kevin's passing:

I remember my parents coming home from a doctor's appointment with bad news. I didn't fully understand what they were talking about and I assumed that it would end up being fine and work out just like it always does. And I especially felt like these types of things don't happen in our family, it's just something you hear about.

I don't remember very many details between when we found out about him and when he was born. As time went on and more things were learned and discussed, I started to understand how serious it was and the reality of the situation. I remember not wanting to talk about it very much, especially with people outside of my family.

I remember the day that Baby Kevin was born, I was at school. I remember being called over the intercom that I was being checked out and my stomach sinking.

The walk to my locker and out to the car was a long one, and I felt super nervous. When we got to the hospital, he was there, and people were taking turns holding him. All the grandparents and Tami and Steve were there. There were lots of tears and lots of hugs.

Normally I would try not to cry and I wasn't into hugs, but that day I didn't care, I couldn't stop crying and the hugs were what I needed.

I remember holding him and not really knowing if he was alive or not. When I look back on this day I usually watch the video Dad made a few years ago and what stands out to me most is that Grandpa Tom seems to me to be the happiest one in the room, he is smiling in most videos and pictures. At first, I thought that was a little weird, but then I realized that he was able to smile that day because he gets it. Grandpa Tom could see God's hand in Baby Kevin, crystal clear.

I remember that we were given the option to stay home from school the next day if we wanted to. I took that option and slept in, I didn't know what to do with myself and kind of didn't want to think about everything that had happened, so I think I spent most of the day playing Call of Duty. When I went back to school, some of the people I was friends with somehow found out about everything that happened and put together a "sorry for your loss" type of card. I wasn't expecting this, especially since I thought no one knew about it, I was pretty thankful for that.

A week later was the funeral, all the crying and the hugging came rushing back. I remember going to the funeral home to take pictures and pick him up. He was put in the back of the suburban in his casket and we headed up to Idaho with the whole extended family. I rode with Gran

dpa Dave and Grandma Linda right behind the suburban, I couldn't help but stare at the back doors of the suburban knowing what was just on the other side. We got there and set up, Jackson and I carried the casket to the grave, everyone was in blue, singing Baby Kevin's song, and letting balloons go.

Afterward, we went to the Dude Ranch Cafe. I remember thinking that that place was a dump, and I was super sad walking in. But everyone else seemed to lighten up a lot more, so between that, endless Mountain Dew, and the food turning out to be some of the best food I've ever had, I started to feel better.

Throughout the entire experience, my parents were good to teach us more specifically about the plan of salvation and how it applied to us in our situation. I didn't fully understand all of it, but it did make me feel better, and it did strengthen my faith. Since then they have continued to teach the plan of salvation, and I have continued to learn about it on my own. Even though this was the hardest thing I've had to go through, the things I have learned through it have been priceless. I'm thankful for my Savior Jesus Christ and His Atonement, and that through Him we can overcome death and in turn be united as a family again.

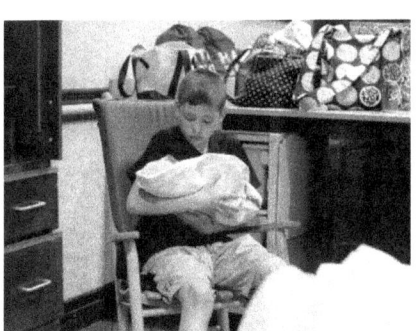

Kloe

Kloe wrote this paper for her Spanish class about six months after her brother died and translated it into english:

My Special Brother

Hi, my name is Kloe I'm going to talk to you about the time I first saw my brother. His name is Kevin but my family calls him Baby Kevin. I'm going to tell you my experience. December 24th, 2011, this was the big day. The day before Christmas is my Mom's birthday and this year we went to Little America for breakfast. When we finished my Mom told us the big news. She was going to have a baby! When we finished our breakfast we went to our house and then my mom asked us who wanted to go to the Dr's office with her. Me, my sister Emmy, and my Dad went with my mom. The Dr couldn't see the baby because he was in a weird position and she couldn't see if he was a boy or girl for sure but she did think there was a 80% chance it was a boy and a 20% chance it was a girl. And that was good news because my family had 5 girls and 2 boys at the time. But the Dr didn't say everything. Two days later we left for Arizona to see our Aunt and Uncle. On January 9th 2012 me and my sister Gracie came home from school and my mom was sitting on her bed crying. She had been back to the Dr and said that it was a boy but he has something called Trisomy 13 and he's probably not going to live but if he does live he'll have lots of problems and it's possible that he could die in her stomach.

May 10th, 2012, Baby Kevin's Birthday

All of my brothers and sisters and me were in school and everyone got the same call that we needed to go home. My Grandma Jan said that we needed to get to the hospital immediately and she drove us all there. She told us something wasn't right with the baby. When we went into the room where my mom was, everyone was crying. My Grandparents were all there and my brother had only lived for one hour and thirty minutes and me and my brother and sisters didn't get to see him alive except for Jackson, my oldest brother. But I did get to hold him and as I was holding him it kept going through my mind how great it would be to be able to take care of him like I helped with Janie and Lilly. I remember thinking for a long time ever since Janie was born how badly I wanted a little brother and all my cousins and my friends all have little brothers and they are so sweet. When my mom said she was having a little boy I was so happy, I can't even explain the feeling, it was so great. But when I got to the hospital and he had died my heart broke and felt like it was gone.

May 19th, 2012, The Funeral

All my family came from the two sides, my Mom's and my Dad's. We buried him in Malad, Idaho with my Great Grandma Ona Moon and her son Boyd who also died as a baby. Me and my sisters and my cousin played a song on our violins. The song was called *I Belong to the Church of Jesus Christ*. After the funeral me and my family sat and talked about how we felt and how much we appreciate each other more and how grateful we are for our Baby Kevin. When we finished we went to go eat at a place called The Dude Ranch. Now every time we go visit Idaho we go visit his grave and we eat at The Dude Ranch. But just because he died doesn't mean we won't see him again or that he won't be a part of our family. Now we have 5 girls and 3 boys. It might be sad that he died but we know we'll see him again. That day I felt sad, happy and a little frustrated. I didn't know it would be so hard losing a brother or sister. When we were at the graveside I guess I didn't really think of how much I loved my family because I was bawling.

And that's the story of my warrior brother and my family has him in our memory and in our hearts every day and we celebrate his life on the 10th of every month.

Gracie

Gracie wrote about her memories of her brother seven years after he passed away:

January 9th, 2012: Going into that hospital room I knew deep down that he wasn't going to live, there wasn't going to be a miracle. But holding him, and being there with all our family I realized he was a miracle. We blew out candles on his tiny cake and sang happy birthday, but when I tried to sing no words came out. I think that's when reality hit me and I started to cry a little.

Papa Tom said a really long prayer, and I tried to pay attention, but my thoughts kept wandering. My mom's best friend Marci was standing right behind me and she had her arms around me, wrapping me in a big hug. She was crying too, and her tears were getting on my head. For the rest of the prayer, all I could think about was Marci's tears falling on my head.

Getting to the grave site was such an odd experience, I had only been there a few times in my life but now

I've been more than I can count. I remember watching Dakota and Jackson carry Baby Kevin's casket to the patch of fake grass a little ways away. Their faces were red and they were both crying. I had never seen my big brothers cry except in the hospital room, but now seeing them so sad just made me sad. I didn't like seeing all the people in my family cry. Especially my big brothers.

I spent the rest of the funeral in and out of tears. I remember feeling Janie grab my arm during the prayer, and normally I would have shrugged her off or got annoyed but I didn't care. I was just glad she was there. There was a lot of hugging during the service. I've never given so many hugs in my life.

I remember taking pictures with the whole family, and not knowing how to hold my violin. It is such an odd shaped instrument to hold elegantly. I was really worried about that, but the picture turned out ok.

I remember exactly where I sat at the Dude Ranch a while later. On the big table in the back on the right-hand side, two seats down, next to Karter. Everyone was so loud. I felt like they needed to be quiet. It didn't feel right to be talking so much after such a nice, reverent service. Karter kept messing around, trying to get me to play sword fight with him with those little plastic swords they put in the sandwiches and making jokes. I wished everyone would be quiet. If we had sat and eaten in complete silence, that would have been perfectly fine with me.

Janie

Janie was three and a half when she lost her baby brother. She doesn't recall very much about that time. She remembers feeling Baby Kevin move in my belly as we'd snuggle together in my rocker. The day he died she remembers her Papa Tom giving the prayer in the hospital and standing with her great grandpa Moon during the graveside service.

Lilly

Lilly has no recollection of Baby Kevin. She was 15 months old when he passed away, but she has always felt close to him. When Lilly was around five years old, and began to understand more about death and loss, she mourned the loss of her brother. Every so often I would find her crying because she was missing her little brother and we would talk about how much he loved her and how lucky she was to have an angel brother watching over her in heaven.

Acknowledgments

Thanks to Kevin and our children for allowing me to share their experiences with the loss of Baby Kevin.

Many thanks to Heather Nan Photography and the nurse who happened to have her camera and took pictures at the hospital until Heather arrived. Thank you to my sister Megan who took photos at the mortuary and graveside service. I will forever treasure the moments they captured.

A huge thank you to all our friends and family who have loved and supported us on our grief journey.

And I thank my Jesus, who not only carried me through my pregnancy and the loss of my son, but has taken all my sorrow and, over time, replaced it with hope, peace, gratitude and joy. I praise Him for His atoning sacrifice, making it possible for me to one day be reunited with my son. I can't wait.

Connect with Becky

Becky was born in
Malad, Idaho, and has
lived in the Salt Lake
Valley most of her life. She
married her high school
sweetheart, Kevin, and
together they have eight
children.

Becky graduated from Utah State University with
a Bachelor of Science in Elementary Education and
currently teaches Seminary part time. She founded
the blog, *What Matters Most* in 2008, where she

journals about her love for God, family and living the gospel of Jesus Christ.

Becky is a Certified Creation Coach with an emphasis on grief coaching. Her online coaching program, *Joy in the Mourning,* helps grieving mothers find peace and healing through Christ as they navigate through their grief journey.

Becky believes everything we experience in this life has purpose, and that a loving and all-knowing God works all things for our good. Her deep faith and trust in her Father in Heaven and His Son, Jesus Christ, guides all that she does. Becky loves being a homemaker, planning vacations, listening to audiobooks while working on a home improvement project, going to lunch with a good friend and spending time with her family.

To learn more about Becky and her grief coaching program scan the QR code or go to her website www.whatmatterswithbeckybeck.com